DOVER·THRIFT·EDITIONS

Selected Poems

PAUL LAURENCE DUNBAR

D1497699

DOVER PUBLICATIONS, INC.
Mineola, New York

DOVER THRIFT EDITIONS

GENERAL EDITOR: PAUL NEGRI

EDITOR OF THIS VOLUME: GLENN MOTT

Bibliographical Note

This new anthology, first published by Dover Publications, Inc. in 1997, contains sixty-eight poems reprinted from standard texts. An introductory Note has been specially prepared for this edition.

Library of Congress Cataloging-in-Publication Data

Dunbar, Paul Laurence, 1872–1906.
[Poems. Selections]
Selected poems / Paul Laurence Dunbar.
    p.   cm. — (Dover thrift editions)
  ISBN 0-486-29980-5 (pbk.)
  I. Title.   II. Series.
PS1556.A4   1997
811'.4—dc21   97-22682
                                                            CIP

Manufactured in the United States of America
Dover Publications, Inc., 31 East 2nd Street, Mineola, N.Y. 11501

Note

PAUL LAURENCE DUNBAR (1872–1906) was born in Dayton, Ohio, and lived primarily in Northern urban environments his entire life. His parents, former Kentucky slaves, divorced when he was four, and he was raised under the tutelage of his mother. He was educated in Dayton public schools, and although Dunbar was often the only black member of his class, he was elected class president and was the founding editor of his high school newspaper. Refused more suitable employment because of his color, he worked as an elevator operator after graduating. His first book, *Oak and Ivy* (1893) was published at his own expense. A second book, *Majors and Minors* (1895) was praised in *Harper's* by William Dean Howells, and Dunbar, a twenty-four year old poet, was suddenly swept into the spotlight by the notice of his obscure volume. Howells subsequently wrote the introduction to Dunbar's first collection, *Lyrics of Lowly Life* (1896).

Dunbar's public success as a poet came at a time when regionalism was the fashion in American literature. The reunion of the country after the Civil War, and the social transformations which that brought about, engendered a widespread interest in poems and stories that were celebrant of regional cultures. The use of dialect was seen as a credible literary device for distinguishing ethnic and provincial character types. Important popularizers of this movement were the midwestern colorists Eugene Field and James Whitcomb Riley, whose tropes Dunbar emulated. In the aftermath of the Reconstruction, an idealized version of the ante-bellum South was particularly well received, and a style of verse emerged from a plantation tradition in which black characters and folkways were nostalgically rendered using Negro dialect. With a reading public that was already under the cultivation of pastoral sentimentalities, writers like Irwin Russell and Joel Chandler Harris minstreled "Negro folk life" to a large popular audience. The underlying race dogma was widely accepted under the cloak of regionalism, and the movement lent plausibility to the humor and pathos of a Southern black persona whose gaze was resolutely fixed in the past.

Dunbar's proximity to poets whose literary blackface defined the meaning of blackness for white culture, has led some readers to place his work within the minstrel tradition and the worst of plantation stereotyping. A response to the name Paul Dunbar is likely to be conditioned by what critic Jean Wagner called "a strange but inevitable feeling of embarrassment." For although his poems helped produce a distinctive black literature, their use of the Southern black literary persona made it impossible for him to respond adequately to the racial conditions he portrayed. Subsequent generations have felt he became a victim of his continued use of a solecistic racial dialect long after it had demonstrated its limitations. Yet Dunbar's ambivalence toward his own dialect poetry has long been a topic of literary historians, and the issues of race and identity in the poetics were as acute for Dunbar as they are for us now. Dunbar lamented his reputation as a dialect poet, because he felt success had come at the expense of his formal poetry in standard literary English. He did not start out as a dialect poet, and told James Weldon Johnson with a tone of self-reproach, "I simply came to the conclusion that I could write it as well, if not better, than anybody else I knew of, and that by doing so I should gain a hearing." Yet there is no reason to think that Dunbar considered his dialect verse inferior to his conventional literary output. He had capitalized on a trend and won a large audience, and though it was often one that felt his verse espoused their own attitudes toward race, neither Dunbar nor black critics of his day thought his dialect poems made black people look ridiculous.

In the 1930s writers of the Harlem Renaissance were warning against using a simplified version of black folklore to win larger audiences. At other times over the past century as well, Dunbar's reputation has changed in accordance with the prospects of African-American culture. In this Dunbar has come to be more of an historical figure than a beloved poet. This is not entirely unreasonable, for while his verse contributed to the articulation of an American vernacular, it exemplifies an historical moment. He was the prototype of a black poet with two separate voices. His verse in literary English, though refined, is often couched in worn romantic idioms, and participates in a sentimental versification characteristic of much of American poetry of the nineteenth century. Notable exceptions to this, like "We Wear the Mask" and "Sympathy," defy the prototypical dilemma by their themes. Though less than half of his verse was written in dialect, the dialect verse has come to be regarded as his most distinctive legacy. His main contribution was the ability to synthesize dialect with a formal and engaging lyricism. The present volume collects the best of Dunbar's musicality and lyrical intensity, found in the likes of "A Negro Love Song," "When Malindy Sings," and "An Anti-Bellum Sermon," poems that seem to break into song when read aloud. The selection is also stylistically varied enough to give a sense of Dunbar's complex historical and literary dimensions, and demonstrates his contribution to the American vernacular.

Contents

Ere Sleep Comes Down to Soothe the Weary Eyes

Ere sleep comes down to soothe the weary eyes,
    Which all the day with ceaseless care have sought
The magic gold which from the seeker flies;
    Ere dreams put on the gown and cap of thought,
And make the waking world a world of lies,—
    Of lies most palpable, uncouth, forlorn,
That say life's full of aches and tears and sighs,—
    Oh, how with more than dreams the soul is torn,
Ere sleep comes down to soothe the weary eyes.

Ere sleep comes down to soothe the weary eyes,
    How all the griefs and heartaches we have known
Come up like pois'nous vapors that arise
    From some base witch's caldron, when the crone,
To work some potent spell, her magic plies.
    The past which held its share of bitter pain,
Whose ghost we prayed that Time might exorcise,
    Comes up, is lived and suffered o'er again,
Ere sleep comes down to soothe the weary eyes.

Ere sleep comes down to soothe the weary eyes,
    What phantoms fill the dimly lighted room;
What ghostly shades in awe-creating guise
    Are bodied forth within the teeming gloom.
What echoes faint of sad and soul-sick cries,
    And pangs of vague inexplicable pain
That pay the spirit's ceaseless enterprise,
    Come thronging through the chambers of the brain,
Ere sleep comes down to soothe the weary eyes.

Ere sleep comes down to soothe the weary eyes,
　　Where ranges forth the spirit far and free?
Through what strange realms and unfamiliar skies
　　Tends her far course to lands of mystery?
To lands unspeakable—beyond surmise,
　　Where shapes unknowable to being spring,
Till, faint of wing, the Fancy fails and dies
　　Much wearied with the spirit's journeying,
Ere sleep comes down to soothe the weary eyes.

Ere sleep comes down to soothe the weary eyes,
　　How questioneth the soul that other soul,—
The inner sense which neither cheats nor lies,
　　But self exposes unto self, a scroll
Full writ with all life's acts unwise or wise,
　　In characters indelible and known;
So, trembling with the shock of sad surprise,
　　The soul doth view its awful self alone,
Ere sleep comes down to soothe the weary eyes.

When sleep comes down to seal the weary eyes,
　　The last dear sleep whose soft embrace is balm,
And whom sad sorrow teaches us to prize
　　For kissing all our passions into calm,
Ah, then, no more we heed the sad world's cries,
　　Or seek to probe th' eternal mystery,
Or fret our souls at long-withheld replies,
　　At glooms through which our visions cannot see,
When sleep comes down to seal the weary eyes.

Accountability

Folks ain't got no right to censuah othah folks about dey habits;
Him dat giv' de squir'ls de bushtails made de bobtails fu' de rabbits.
Him dat built de gread big mountains hollered out de little valleys,
Him dat made de streets an' driveways wasn't shamed to make de
　　alleys.

We is all constructed diff'ent, d'ain't no two of us de same;
We cain't he'p ouah likes an' dislikes, ef we'se bad we ain't to blame.

Ef we'se good, we needn't show off, case you bet it ain't ouah doin'
We gits into su'ttain channels dat we jes' cain't he'p pu'suin'.

But we all fits into places dat no othah ones could fill,
An' we does the things we has to, big er little, good er ill.
John cain't tek de place o' Henry, Su an' Sally ain't alike;
Bass ain't nuthin' like a suckah, chub ain't nuthin' like a pike.

When you come to think about it, how it's all planned out it's splen-
    did.
Nuthin's done er evah happens, 'dout hit's somefin' dat's intended;
Don't keer whut you does, you has to, an' hit sholy beats de dick-
    ens,—
Viney, go put on de kittle, I got one o' mastah's chickens.

Life

A crust of bread and a corner to sleep in,
A minute to smile and an hour to weep in,
A pint of joy to a peck of trouble,
And never a laugh but the moans come double;
        And that is life!

A crust and a corner that love makes precious,
With a smile to warm and the tears to refresh us;
And joy seems sweeter when cares come after,
And a moan is the finest of foils for laughter;
        And that is life!

An Ante-Bellum Sermon

We is gathahed hyeah, my brothahs,
    In dis howlin' wildaness,
Fu' to speak some words of comfo't
    To each othah in distress.
An' we chooses fu' ouah subjic'
    Dis—we'll 'splain it by an' by;
"An' de Lawd said, 'Moses, Moses,'

An' de man said, 'Hyeah am I.'"

Now ole Pher'oh, down in Egypt,
  Was de wuss man evah bo'n,
An' he had de Hebrew chillun
  Down dah wukin' in his co'n;
'Twell de Lawd got tiahed o' his foolin',
  An' sez he: "I'll let him know—
Look hyeah, Moses, go tell Pher'oh
  Fu' to let dem chillun go."

"An' ef he refuse to do it,
  I will make him rue de houah,
Fu' I'll empty down on Egypt
  All de vials of my powah."
Yes, he did—an' Pher'oh's ahmy
  Wasn't wuth a ha'f a dime;
Fu' de Lawd will he'p his chillun,
  You kin trust him evah time.

An' yo' enemies may 'sail you
  In de back an' in de front;
But de Lawd is all aroun' you,
  Fu' to ba' de battle's brunt.
Dey kin fo'ge yo' chains an' shackles
  F'om de mountains to de sea;
But de Lawd will sen' some Moses
  Fu' to set his chillun free.

An' de lan' shall hyeah his thundah,
  Lak a blas' f'om Gab'el's ho'n,
Fu' de Lawd of hosts is mighty
  When he girds his ahmor on.
But fu' feah some one mistakes me,
  I will pause right hyeah to say,
Dat I'm still a-preachin' ancient,
  I ain't talkin' 'bout to-day.

But I tell you, fellah christuns,
  Things'll happen mighty strange;
Now, de Lawd done dis fu' Isrul,

An' his ways don't nevah change,
An' de love he showed to Isrul
    Wasn't all on Isrul spent;
Now don't run an' tell yo' mastahs
    Dat I's preachin' discontent.

'Cause I isn't; I'se a-judgin'
    Bible people by deir ac's;
I'se a-givin' you de Scriptuah,
    I'se a-handin' you de fac's.
Cose ole Pher'oh b'lieved in slav'ry,
    But de Lawd he let him see,
Dat de people he put bref in,—
    Evah mothah's son was free.

An' dah's othahs thinks lak Pher'oh,
    But dey calls de Scriptuah liar,
Fu' de Bible says "a servant
    Is a-worthy of his hire."
An' you cain't git roun' nor thoo dat,
    An' you cain't git ovah it,
Fu' whatevah place you git in,
    Dis hyeah Bible too'll fit.

So you see de Lawd's intention,
    Evah sence de worl' began,
Was dat His almighty freedom
    Should belong to evah man,
But I think it would be bettah,
    Ef I'd pause agin to say,
Dat I'm talkin' 'bout ouah freedom
    In a Bibleistic way.

But de Moses is a-comin',
    An' he's comin', suah and fas'
We kin hyeah his feet a-trompin',
    We kin hyeah his trumpit blas'.
But I want to wa'n you people,
    Don't you git too brigity;
An' don't you git to braggin'
    'Bout dese things, you wait an' see.

But when Moses wif his powah
   Comes an' sets us chillun free,
We will praise de gracious Mastah
   Dat has gin us liberty;
An' we'll shout ouah halleluyahs,
   On dat mighty reck'nin' day,
When we'se reco'nised ez citiz'—
   Huh uh! Chillun, let us pray!

Ode to Ethiopia

O Mother Race! to thee I bring
This pledge of faith unwavering,
   This tribute to thy glory.
I know the pangs which thou didst feel,
When Slavery crushed thee with its heel,
   With thy dear blood all gory.

Sad days were those—ah, sad indeed!
But through the land the fruitful seed
   Of better times was growing.
The plant of freedom upward sprung,
And spread its leaves so fresh and young—
   Its blossoms now are blowing.

On every hand in this fair land,
Proud Ethiope's swarthy children stand
   Beside their fairer neighbour;
The forests flee before their stroke,
Their hammers ring, their forges smoke,—
   They stir in honest labour.

They tread the fields where honour calls;
Their voices sound through senate halls
   In majesty and power.
To right they cling; the hymns they sing
Up to the skies in beauty ring,
   And bolder grow each hour.

Be proud, my Race, in mind and soul;
Thy name is writ on Glory's scroll
   In characters of fire.
High 'mid the clouds of Fame's bright sky
Thy banner's blazoned folds now fly,
   And truth shall lift them higher.

Thou hast the right to noble pride,
Whose spotless robes were purified
   By blood's severe baptism.
Upon thy brow the cross was laid,
And labour's painful sweat-beads made
   A consecrating chrism.

No other race, or white or black,
When bound as thou wert, to the rack,
   So seldom stooped to grieving;
No other race, when free again,
Forgot the past and proved them men
   So noble in forgiving.

Go on and up! Our souls and eyes
Shall follow thy continuous rise;
   Our ears shall list thy story
From bards who from thy root shall spring,
And proudly tune their lyres to sing
   Of Ethiopia's glory.

The Mystery

I was not; now I am—a few days hence
I shall not be; I fain would look before
And after, but can neither do; some Power
Or lack of power says "no" to all I would.
I stand upon a wide and sunless plain,
Nor chart nor steel to guide my steps aright.
Whene'er, o'ercoming fear, I dare to move,
I grope without direction and by chance.
Some feign to hear a voice and feel a hand

That draws them ever upward thro' the gloom.
But I—I hear no voice and touch no hand,
Tho' oft thro' silence infinite I list,
And strain my hearing to supernal sounds;
Tho' oft thro' fateful darkness do I reach,
And stretch my hand to find that other hand.
I question of th' eternal bending skies
That seem to neighbor with the novice earth;
But they roll on, and daily shut their eyes
On me, as I one day shall do on them,
And tell me not the secret that I ask.

Not They Who Soar

Not they who soar, but they who plod
Their rugged way, unhelped, to God
Are heroes; they who higher fare,
And, flying, fan the upper air,
Miss all the toil that hugs the sod.
'Tis they whose backs have felt the rod,
Whose feet have pressed the path unshod,
May smile upon defeated care,
            Not they who soar.

High up there are no thorns to prod,
Nor boulders lurking 'neath the clod
To turn the keenness of the share,
For flight is ever free and rare;
But heroes they the soil who've trod,
            Not they who soar!

A Banjo Song

Oh, dere's lots o' keer an' trouble
        In dis world to swaller down;
An' ol' Sorrer's purty lively
        In her way o' gittin' roun'.
Yet dere's times when I furgit 'em,—
        Aches an' pains an' troubles all,—

An' it's when I tek at ebenin'
   My ol' banjo f'om de wall.

'Bout de time dat night is fallin'
   An' my daily wu'k is done,
An' above de shady hilltops
   I kin see de settin' sun;
When de quiet, restful shadders
   Is beginnin' jes' to fall, —
Den I take de little banjo
   F'om its place upon de wall.

Den my fam'ly gadders roun' me
   In de fadin' o' de light,
Ez I strike de strings to try 'em
   Ef dey all is tuned er-right.
An' it seems we're so nigh heaben
   We kin hyeah de angels sing
When de music o' dat banjo
   Sets my cabin all er-ring.

An' my wife an' all de othahs, —
   Male an' female, small an' big, —
Even up to gray-haired granny,
   Seems jes' boun' to do a jig;
'Twell I change de style o' music,
   Change de movement an' de time,
An' de ringin' little banjo
   Plays an ol' hea't-feelin' hime.

An' somehow my th'oat gits choky,
   An' a lump keeps tryin' to rise
Lak it wan'ed to ketch de water
   Dat was flowin' to my eyes;
An' I feel dat I could sorter
   Knock de socks clean off o' sin
Ez I hyeah my po' ol' granny
   Wif huh tremblin' voice jine in.

Den we all th'ow in our voices
   Fu' to he'p de chune out too,

Lak a big camp-meetin' choiry
    Tryin' to sing a mou'nah th'oo.
An' our th'oahts let out de music,
    Sweet an' solemn, loud an' free,
'Twell de raftahs o' my cabin
    Echo wif de melody.

Oh, de music o' de banjo,
    Quick an' deb'lish, solemn, slow,
Is de greates' joy an' solace
    Dat a weary slave kin know!
So jes' let me hyeah it ringin',
    Dough de chune be po' an' rough,
It's a pleasure; an' de pleasures
    O' dis life is few enough.

Now, de blessed little angels
    Up in heaben, we are told,
Don't do nothin' all dere lifetime
    'Ceptin' play on ha'ps o' gold.
Now I think heaben'd be mo' homelike
    Ef we'd hyeah some music fall
F'om a real ol'-fashioned banjo,
    Like dat one upon de wall.

Unexpressed

Deep in my heart that aches with the repression,
    And strives with plenitude of bitter pain,
There lives a thought that clamors for expression,
    And spends its undelivered force in vain.

What boots it that some other may have thought it?
    The right of thoughts' expression is divine;
The price of pain I pay for it has bought it,
    I care not who lays claim to it—'t is mine!

And yet not mine until it be delivered;
    The manner of its birth shall prove the test.

Alas, alas, my rock of pride is shivered—
    I beat my brow—the thought still unexpressed.

Song of Summer

Dis is gospel weathah sho'—
    Hills is sawt o' hazy.
Meddahs level ez a flo'
    Callin' to de lazy.
Sky all white wif streaks o' blue,
    Sunshine softly gleamin',
D'ain't no wuk hit's right to do,
    Nothin' 's right but dreamin'.

Dreamin' by de rivah side
    Wif de watahs glist'nin',
Feelin' good an' satisfied
    Ez you lay a-list'nin'
To the little nakid boys
    Splashin' in de watah,
Hollerin' fu' to spress deir joys
    Jes' lak youngsters ought to.

Squir'l a-tippin' on his toes,
    So's to hide an' view you;
Whole flocks o' camp-meetin' crows
    Shoutin' hallelujah.
Peckahwood erpon de tree
    Tappin' lak a hammah;
Jaybird chattin' wif a bee,
    Tryin' to teach him grammah.

Breeze is blowin' wif perfume,
    Jes' enough to tease you;
Hollyhocks is all in bloom,
    Smellin' fu' to please you.
Go 'way, folks, an' let me 'lone,
    Times is gettin' dearah—
Summah's settin' on de th'one,
    An' I'm a-layin' neah huh!

Religion

I am no priest of crooks nor creeds,
For human wants and human needs
Are more to me than prophets' deeds;
And human tears and human cares
Affect me more than human prayers.

Go, cease your wail, lugubrious saint!
You fret high Heaven with your plaint.
Is this the "Christian's joy" you paint?
Is this the Christian's boasted bliss?
Avails your faith no more than this?

Take up your arms, come out with me,
Let Heav'n alone; humanity
Needs more and Heaven less from thee.
With pity for mankind look 'round;
Help them to rise—and Heaven is found.

The Colored Soldiers

If the muse were mine to tempt it
   And my feeble voice were strong,
If my tongue were trained to measures,
   I would sing a stirring song.
I would sing a song heroic
   Of those noble sons of Ham,
Of the gallant colored soldiers
   Who fought for Uncle Sam!

In the early days you scorned them,
   And with many a flip and flout
Said "These battles are the white man's,
   And the whites will fight them out."
Up the hills you fought and faltered,
   In the vales you strove and bled,
While your ears still heard the thunder
   Of the foes' advancing tread.

Then distress fell on the nation,
    And the flag was drooping low;
Should the dust pollute your banner?
    No! the nation shouted, No!
So when War, in savage triumph,
    Spread abroad his funeral pall—
Then you called the colored soldiers,
    And they answered to your call.

And like hounds unleashed and eager
    For the life blood of the prey,
Sprung they forth and bore them bravely
    In the thickest of the fray.
And where'er the fight was hottest,
    Where the bullets fastest fell,
There they pressed unblanched and fearless
    At the very mouth of hell.

Ah, they rallied to the standard
    To uphold it by their might;
None were stronger in the labors,
    None were braver in the fight.
From the blazing breach of Wagner
    To the plains of Olustee,
They were foremost in the fight
    Of the battles of the free.

And at Pillow! God have mercy
    On the deeds committed there,
And the souls of those poor victims
    Sent to Thee without a prayer.
Let the fulness of Thy pity
    O'er the hot wrought spirits sway
Of the gallant colored soldiers
    Who fell fighting on that day!

Yes, the Blacks enjoy their freedom,
    And they won it dearly, too;
For the life blood of their thousands
    Did the southern fields bedew.
In the darkness of their bondage,

In the depths of slavery's night,
Their muskets flashed the dawning,
    And they fought their way to light.

They were comrades then and brothers,
    Are they more or less to-day?
They were good to stop a bullet
    And to front the fearful fray.
They were citizens and soldiers,
    When rebellion raised its head;
And the traits that made them worthy,—
    Ah! those virtues are not dead.

They have shared your nightly vigils,
    They have shared your daily toil;
And their blood with yours commingling
    Has enriched the Southern soil.
They have slept and marched and suffered
    'Neath the same dark skies as you,
They have met as fierce a foeman,
    And have been as brave and true.

And their deeds shall find a record
    In the registry of Fame;
For their blood has cleansed completely
    Every blot of Slavery's shame.
So all honor and all glory
    To those noble sons of Ham—
The gallant colored soldiers
    Who fought for Uncle Sam!

When De Co'n Pone's Hot

Dey is times in life when Nature
    Seems to slip a cog an' go,
Jes' a-rattlin' down creation,
    Lak an ocean's overflow;
When de worl' jes' stahts a-spinnin'
    Lak a picanniny's top,

An' yo' cup o' joy is brimmin'
  'Twell it seems about to slop,
An' you feel jes' lak a racah,
  Dat is trainin' fu' to trot—
When yo' mammy says de blessin'
  An' de co'n pone's hot.

When you set down at de table,
  Kin' o' weary lak an' sad,
An' you'se jes' a little tiahed
  An' purhaps a little mad;
How yo' gloom tu'ns into gladness,
  How yo' joy drives out de doubt
When de oven do' is opened,
  An' de smell comes po'in' out;
Why, de 'lectric light o' Heaven
  Seems to settle on de spot,
When yo' mammy says de blessin'
  An' de co'n pone's hot.

When de cabbage pot is steamin'
  An' de bacon good an' fat,
When de chittlins is a-sputter'n'
  So's to show you whah dey's at;
Tek away yo' sody biscuit,
  Tek away yo' cake an' pie,
Fu' de glory time is comin',
  An' it's 'proachin' mighty nigh,
An' you want to jump an' hollah,
  Dough you know you'd bettah not,
When yo' mammy says de blessin'
  An' de co'n pone's hot.

I have hyeahd o' lots o' sermons,
  An' I've hyeahd o' lots o' prayers,
An' I've listened to some singin'
  Dat has tuck me up de stairs
Of de Glory-Lan' an' set me
  Jes' below de Mastah's th'one,
An' have lef' my hea't a-singin'
  In a happy aftah tone;

But dem wu'ds so sweetly murmured
    Seem to tech de softes' spot,
When my mammy says de blessin',
    An' de co'n pone's hot.

Discovered

Seen you down at chu'ch las' night,
    Nevah min', Miss Lucy.
What I mean? oh, dat's all right,
    Nevah min', Miss Lucy.
You was sma't ez sma't could be,
But you couldn't hide f'om me.
Ain't I got two eyes to see!
    Nevah min', Miss Lucy.

Guess you thought you's awful keen;
    Nevah min', Miss Lucy.
Evahthing you done, I seen;
    Nevah min', Miss Lucy.
Seen him tek yo' ahm jes' so,
When he got outside de do'—
Oh, I know dat man's yo' beau!
    Nevah min', Miss Lucy.

Say now, honey, wha'd he say?—
    Nevah min', Miss Lucy!
Keep yo' secrets—dat's yo' way—
    Nevah min', Miss Lucy.
Won't tell me an' I'm yo' pal—
I'm gwine tell his othah gal,—
Know huh, too, huh name is Sal;
    Nevah min', Miss Lucy!

A Summer's Night

The night is dewy as a maiden's mouth,
    The skies are bright as are a maiden's eyes,

Soft as a maiden's breath the wind that flies
Up from the perfumed bosom of the South.
Like sentinels, the pines stand in the park;
  And hither hastening, like rakes that roam,
  With lamps to light their wayward footsteps home,
The fireflies come stagg'ring down the dark.

Ships That Pass in the Night

Out in the sky the great dark clouds are massing;
  I look far out into the pregnant night,
Where I can hear a solemn booming gun
  And catch the gleaming of a random light,
That tells me that the ship I seek is passing, passing.

My tearful eyes my soul's deep hurt are glassing;
  For I would hail and check that ship of ships.
I stretch my hands imploring, cry aloud,
  My voice falls dead a foot from mine own lips,
And but its ghost doth reach that vessel, passing, passing.

O Earth, O Sky, O Ocean, both surpassing,
  O heart of mine, O soul that dreads the dark!
Is there no hope for me? Is there no way
  That I may sight and check that speeding bark
Which out of sight and sound is passing, passing?

We Wear the Mask

We wear the mask that grins and lies,
It hides our cheeks and shades our eyes,—
This debt we pay to human guile;
With torn and bleeding hearts we smile,
And mouth with myriad subtleties.

Why should the world be overwise,
In counting all our tears and sighs?

Nay, let them only see us, while
    We wear the mask.

We smile, but, O great Christ, our cries
To thee from tortured souls arise.
We sing, but oh the clay is vile
Beneath our feet, and long the mile;
But let the world dream otherwise,
    We wear the mask!

A Negro Love Song

Seen my lady home las' night,
    Jump back, honey, jump back.
Hel' huh han' an' sque'z it tight,
    Jump back, honey, jump back.
Hyeahd huh sigh a little sigh,
Seen a light gleam f'om huh eye,
An' a smile go flittin' by—
    Jump back, honey, jump back.

Hyeahd de win' blow thoo de pine,
    Jump back, honey, jump back.
Mockin'-bird was singin' fine,
    Jump back, honey, jump back.
An' my hea't was beatin' so,
When I reached my lady's do',
Dat I couldn't ba' to go—
    Jump back, honey, jump back.

Put my ahm aroun' huh wais',
    Jump back, honey, jump back.
Raised huh lips an' took a tase,
    Jump back, honey, jump back.
Love me, honey, love me true?
Love me well ez I love you?
An' she answe'd, "'Cose I do"—
    Jump back, honey, jump back.

If

If life were but a dream, my Love,
    And death the waking time;
If day had not a beam, my Love,
    And night had not a rhyme,—
        A barren, barren world were this
        Without one saving gleam;
        I'd only ask that with a kiss
        You'd wake me from the dream.

If dreaming were the sum of days,
    And loving were the bane;
If battling for a wreath of bays
    Could soothe a heart in pain,—
        I'd scorn the meed of battle's might,
        All other aims above
        I'd choose the human's higher right,
        To suffer and to love!

Signs of the Times

Air a-gittin' cool an' coolah,
    Frost a-comin' in de night,
Hicka' nuts an' wa'nuts fallin',
    Possum keepin' out o' sight.
Tu'key struttin' in de ba'nya'd,
    Nary step so proud ez his;
Keep on struttin', Mistah Tu'key,
    Yo' do' know whut time it is.

Cidah press commence a-squeakin',
    Eatin' apples sto'ed away,
Chillun swa'min' 'roun' lak ho'nets,
    Huntin' aigs ermung de hay.
Mistah Tu'key keep on gobblin'
    At de geese a-flyin' souf,
Oomph: dat bird do' know whut's comin';
    Ef he did he'd shet his mouf.

Pumpkin gittin' good an' yallah
    Mek me open up my eyes;
Seems lak it's a-lookin' at me
    Jes' a-la'in' dah sayin' "Pies."
Tu'key gobbler gwine 'roun' blowin',
    Gwine 'roun' gibbin' sass an' slack;
Keep on talkin', Mistah Tu'key,
    You ain't seed no almanac.

Fa'mer walkin' th'oo de ba'nya'd
    Seein' how things is comin' on,
Sees ef all de fowls is fatt'nin'—
    Good times comin' sho's you bo'n.
Hyeahs dat tu'key gobbler braggin',
    Den his face break in a smile—
Nebbah min', you sassy rascal,
    He's gwine nab you atter while.

Choppin' suet in de kitchen,
    Stonin' raisins in de hall,
Beef a-cookin' fu' de mince meat,
    Spices groun'—I smell 'em all.
Look hyeah, Tu'key, stop dat gobblin',
    You ain' luned de sense ob feah,
You ol' fool, yo' naik's in dangah,
    Do' you know Thanksgibbin's hyeah?

Why Fades a Dream?

Why fades a dream?
    An iridescent ray
Flecked in between the tryst
    Of night and day.
    Why fades a dream?—
Of consciousness the shade
Wrought out by lack of light and made
    Upon life's stream.
    Why fades a dream?

That thought may thrive,
   So fades the fleshless dream;
Lest men should learn to trust
   The things that seem.
   So fades a dream,
That living thought may grow
And like a waxing star-beam glow
   Upon life's stream—
   So fades a dream.

When Malindy Sings

G'way an' quit dat noise, Miss Lucy—
   Put dat music book away;
What's de use to keep on tryin'?
   Ef you practise twell you're gray,
You cain't sta't no notes a-flyin'
   Lak de ones dat rants and rings
F'om de kitchen to de big woods
   When Malindy sings.

You ain't got de nachel o'gans
   Fu' to make de soun' come right,
You ain't got de tu'ns an' twistin's
   Fu' to make it sweet an' light.
Tell you one thing now, Miss Lucy,
   An' I'm tellin' you fu' true,
When hit comes to raal right singin',
   'T ain't no easy thing to do.

Easy 'nough fu' folks to hollah,
   Lookin' at de lines an' dots,
When dey ain't no one kin sence it,
   An' de chune comes in, in spots;
But fu' real melojous music,
   Dat jes' strikes you' hea't and clings,
Jes' you stan' an' listen wif me
   When Malindy sings.

Ain't you nevah hyeahd Malindy?
   Blessed soul, tek up de cross!
Look hyeah, ain't you jokin', honey?
   Well, you don't know whut you los'.
Y' ought to hyeah dat gal a-wa'blin',
   Robins, la'ks, an' all dem things,
Heish dey moufs an' hides dey faces
   When Malindy sings.

Fiddlin' man jes' stop his fiddlin',
   Lay his fiddle on de she'f;
Mockin'-bird quit tryin' to whistle,
   'Cause he jes' so shamed hisse'f.
Folks a-playin' on de banjo
   Draps dey fingahs on de strings—
Bless yo' soul—fu'gits to move 'em,
   When Malindy sings.

She jes' spreads huh mouf and hollahs,
   "Come to Jesus," twell you hyeah
Sinnahs' tremblin' steps and voices,
   Timid-lak a-drawin' neah;
Den she tu'ns to "Rock of Ages,"
   Simply to de cross she clings,
An' you fin' yo' teahs a-drappin'
   When Malindy sings.

Who dat says dat humble praises
   Wif de Master nevah counts?
Heish yo' mouf, I hyeah dat music,
   Ez hit rises up an' mounts—
Floatin' by de hills an' valleys,
   Way above dis buryin' sod,
Ez hit makes its way in glory
   To de very gates of God!

Oh, hit's sweetah dan de music
   Of an edicated band;
An' hit's dearah dan de battle's
   Song o' triumph in de lan'.
It seems holier dan evenin'

When de solemn chu'ch bell rings,
    Ez I sit an' ca'mly listen
        While Malindy sings.

Towsah, stop dat ba'kin', hyeah me!
    Mandy, mek dat chile keep still;
Don't you hyeah de echoes callin'
    F'om de valley to de hill?
Let me listen, I can hyeah it,
    Th'oo de bresh of angels' wings,
Sof' an' sweet, "Swing Low, Sweet Chariot,"
    Ez Malindy sings.

The Party

Dey had a gread big pahty down to Tom's de othah night;
Was I dah? You bet! I nevah in my life see sich a sight;
All de folks f'om fou' plantations was invited, an' dey come,
Dey come troopin' thick ez chillun when dey hyeahs a fife an' drum.
Evahbody dressed deir fines'—Heish yo' mouf an' git away,
Aint' seen no sich fancy dressin' sence las' quah'tly meetin' day;
Gals all dressed in silks an' satins, not a wrinkle ner a crease,
Eyes a-battin', teeth a-shinin', haih breshed back ez slick ez grease;
Sku'ts all tucked an' puffed an' ruffled, evah blessed seam an' stitch;
Ef you'd seen 'em wif deir mistus, couldn't swahed to which was which.
Men all dressed up in Prince Alberts, swaller-tails 'u'd tek yo' bref!
I cain't tell you nothin' 'bout it, y' ought to see it fu' yo'se'f.
Who was dah? Now who you askin'? How you 'spect I gwine to know?
You mus' think I stood an' counted evahbody at de do'.
Ole man Babah's house-boy Isaac, brung dat gal, Malindy Jane,
Huh a-hangin' to his elbow, him a-struttin' wif a cane;
My, but Hahvey Jones was jealous! seemed to stick him lak a tho'n;
But he laughed with Viney Cahteh, tryin' ha'd to not let on,
But a pusson would 'a' noticed f'om de d'rection of his look,
Dat he was watchin' ev'ry step dat Ike an' Lindy took.
Ike he foun' a cheer an' asked huh: "Won't you set down?" wif a smile,
An' she answe'd up a-bowin', "Oh, I reckon 't ain't wuth while."
Dat was jes' fu' style, I reckon, 'cause she sot down jes' de same,
An' she stayed dah 'twell he fetched huh fu' to jine some so't o' game;

Den I hyeahd huh sayin' propah, ez she riz to go away,
"Oh, you raly mus' excuse me, fu' I hardly keers to play."
But I seen huh in a minute wif de othahs on de flo',
An' dah wasn't any one o' dem a-playin' any mo';
Comin' down de flo' a-bowin' an' a-swayin' an' a-swingin',
Puttin' on huh high–toned mannah all de time dat she was singin':
"Oh, swing Johnny up an' down, swing him all aroun',
Swing Johnny up an' down, swing him all aroun',
Oh, swing Johnny up an' down, swing him all aroun'
Fa' you well, my dahlin'."
Had to laff at ole man Johnson, he's a caution now, you bet—
Hittin' clost onto a hunderd, but he's spry an' nimble yet;
He 'lowed how a-so't o' gigglin', "I ain't ole, I'll let you see,
D' ain't no use in gittin' feeble, now you youngstahs jes' watch me,"
An' he grabbed ole Aunt Marier—weighs th'ee hunderd mo' er less,
An' he spun huh 'roun' de cabin swingin' Johnny lak de res'.
Evahbody laffed an' hollahed: "Go it! Swing huh, Uncle Jim!"
An' he swung huh too, I reckon, lak a youngstah, who but him.
Dat was bettah'n young Scott Thomas, tryin' to be so awful smaht.
You know when dey gits to singin' an' dey comes to dat ere paht:
          "In some lady's new brick house,
      In some lady's gyahden.
          Ef you don't let me out, I will jump out,
      So fa' you well, my dahlin'."
Den dey's got a circle 'roun' you, an' you's got to break de line;
Well, dat dahky was so anxious, lak to bust hisse'f a-tryin';
Kep' on blund'rin' 'roun' an' foolin' 'twell he giv' one gread big jump,
Broke de line, an' lit head-fo'most in de fiah-place right plump;
Hit 'ad fiah in it, mind you; well, I thought my soul I'd bust,
Tried my best to keep f'om laffin', but hit seemed like die I must!
Y' ought to seen dat man a-scramblin' f'om de ashes an' de grime.
Did it bu'n him! Sich a question, why he didn't give it time;
Th'ow'd dem ashes and dem cindahs evah which-a-way I guess,
An' you nevah did, I reckon, clap yo' eyes on sich a mess;
Fu' he sholy made a picter an' a funny one to boot,
Wif his clothes all full o' ashes an' his face all full o' soot.
Well, hit laked to stopped de pahty, an' I reckon lak ez not
Dat it would ef Tom's wife, Mandy, hadn't happened on de spot,
To invite us out to suppah—well, we scrambled to de table,
An' I'd lak to tell you 'bout it—what we had—but I ain't able,
Mention jes' a few things, dough I know I hadn't orter,

Fu' I know 't will staht a hank'rin' an' yo' mouf'll 'mence to worter.
We had wheat bread white ez cotton an' a egg pone jes' like gol',
Hog jole, bilin' hot an' steamin' roasted shoat an' ham sliced cold—
Look out! What's de mattah wif you? Don't be fallin' on de flo';
Ef it's go'n' to 'fect you dat way, I won't tell you nothin' mo'.
Dah now—well, we had hot chittlin's—now you's tryin' ag'in to fall,
Cain't you stan' to hyeah about it? S'pose you'd been an' seed it all;
Seed dem gread big sweet pertaters, layin' by de possum's side,
Seed dat coon in all his gravy, reckon den you'd up and died!
Mandy 'lowed "you all mus' 'scuse me, d' wa'n't much upon my
        she'ves,
But I's done my bes' to suit you, so set down an' he'p yo'se'ves."
Tom, he 'lowed: "I don't b'lieve in 'pologisin' an' perfessin',
Let 'em tek it lak dey ketch it. Eldah Thompson, ask de blessin'.'"
Wish you'd seed dat colo'ed preachah cleah his th'oat an' bow his
        head;
One eye shet, an' one eye open,—dis is evah wud he said:
"Lawd, look down in tendah mussy on sich generous hea'ts ez dese;
Make us truly thankful, amen. Pass dat possum, ef you please!"
Well, we eat and drunk ouah po'tion, 'twell dah wasn't nothin' lef',
An' we felt jes' like new sausage, we was mos' nigh stuffed to def!
Tom, he knowed how we'd be feelin', so he had de fiddlah 'roun',
An' he made us cleah de cabin fu' to dance dat suppah down.
Jim, de fiddlah, chuned his fiddle, put some rosum on his bow,
Set a pine box on de table, mounted it an' let huh go!
He's a fiddlah, now I tell you, an' he made dat fiddle ring,
'Twell de ol'est an' de lamest had to give deir feet a fling.
Jigs, cotillions, reels an' breakdowns, cordrills an' a waltz er two;
Bless yo' soul, dat music winged 'em an' dem people lak to flew.
Cripple Joe, de old rheumatic, danced dat flo' f'om side to middle,
Th'owed away his crutch an' hopped it; what's rheumatics 'ginst a fid-
        dle?
Eldah Thompson got so tickled dat he lak to los' his grace,
Had to tek bofe feet an' hol' dem so's to keep 'em in deir place.
An' de Christuns an' de sinnahs got so mixed up on dat flo',
Dat I don't see how dey'd pahted ef de trump had chanced to blow.
Well, we danced dat way an' capahed in de mos' redic'lous way,
'Twell de roostahs in de bahnyard cleahed deir th'oats an' crowed fu'
        day.
Y' ought to been dah, fu' I tell you evahthing was rich an' prime,
An' dey ain't no use in talkin' we jes' had one scrumptious time!

Her Thought and His

The gray of the sea, and the gray of the sky,
A glimpse of the moon like a half-closed eye.
The gleam on the waves and the light on the land,
A thrill in my heart,—and—my sweetheart's hand.

She turned from the sea with a woman's grace,
And the light fell soft on her upturned face,
And I thought of the flood-tide of infinite bliss
That would flow to my heart from a single kiss.

But my sweetheart was shy, so I dared not ask
For the boon, so bravely I wore the mask.
But into her face there came a flame:—
I wonder could she have been thinking the same?

The Right to Die

I have no fancy for that ancient cant
That makes us masters of our destinies,
And not our lives, to hold or give them up
As will directs; I cannot, will not think
That men, the subtle worms, who plot and plan
And scheme and calculate with such shrewd wit,
Are such great blund'ring fools as not to know
When they have lived enough.
                    Men court not death
When there are sweets still left in life to taste.
Nor will a brave man choose to live when he,
Full deeply drunk of life, has reached the dregs,
And knows that now but bitterness remains.
He is the coward who, outfaced in this,
Fears the false goblins of another life.
I honor him who being much harassed
Drinks of sweet courage until drunk of it,—
Then seizing Death, reluctant, by the hand,
Leaps with him, fearless, to eternal peace!

Behind the Arras

As in some dim baronial hall restrained,
A prisoner sits, engirt by secret doors
And waving tapestries that argue forth
Strange passages into the outer air;
So in this dimmer room which we call life,
Thus sits the soul and marks with eye intent
That mystic curtain o'er the portal death;
Still deeming that behind the arras lies
The lambent way that leads to lasting light.
Poor fooled and foolish soul! Know now that death
Is but a blind, false door that nowhere leads,
And gives no hope of exit final, free.

A Hymn

After Reading "Lead, Kindly Light"

Lead gently, Lord, and slow,
    For oh, my steps are weak,
And ever as I go,
    Some soothing sentence speak;

That I may turn my face
    Through doubt's obscurity
Toward thine abiding-place,
    E'en tho' I cannot see.

For lo, the way is dark;
    Through mist and cloud I grope,
Save for that fitful spark,
    The little flame of hope.

Lead gently, Lord, and slow,
    For fear that I may fall;
I know not where to go
    Unless I hear thy call.

My fainting soul doth yearn
   For thy green hills afar;
So let thy mercy burn—
   My greater, guiding star!

Sympathy

I know what the caged bird feels, alas!
   When the sun is bright on the upland slopes;
When the wind stirs soft through the springing grass,
And the river flows like a stream of glass;
   When the first bird sings and the first bud opes,
And the faint perfume from its chalice steals—
I know what the caged bird feels!

I know why the caged bird beats his wing
   Till its blood is red on the cruel bars;
For he must fly back to his perch and cling
When he fain would be on the bough a-swing;
   And a pain still throbs in the old, old scars
And they pulse again with a keener sting—
I know why he beats his wing!

I know why the caged bird sings, ah me,
   When his wing is bruised and his bosom sore,—
When he beats his bars and he would be free;
It is not a carol of joy or glee,
   But a prayer that he sends from his heart's deep core,
But a plea, that upward to Heaven he flings—
I know why the caged bird sings!

Little Brown Baby

Little brown baby wif spa'klin' eyes,
   Come to yo' pappy an' set on his knee.
What you been doin', suh—makin' san' pies?
   Look at dat bib—you's ez du'ty ez me.

Look at dat mouf—dat's merlasses, I bet;
   Come hyeah, Maria, an' wipe off his han's.
Bees gwine to ketch you an' eat you up yit,
   Bein' so sticky an' sweet—goodness lan's!

Little brown baby wif spa'klin' eyes,
   Who's pappy's darlin' an' who's pappy's chile?
Who is it all de day nevah once tries
   Fu' to be cross, er once loses dat smile?
Whah did you git dem teef? My, you's a scamp!
   Whah did dat dimple come f'om in yo' chin?
Pappy do' know you—I b'lieves you's a tramp;
   Mammy, dis hyeah's some ol' straggler got in!

Let's th'ow him outen de do' in de san',
   We do' want stragglers a-layin' 'roun' hyeah;
Let's gin him 'way to de big buggah-man;
   I know he's hidin' erroun' hyeah right neah.
Buggah-man, buggah-man, come in de do',
   Hyeah's a bad boy you kin have fu' to eat.
Mammy an' pappy do' want him no mo',
   Swaller him down f'om his haid to his feet!

Dah, now, I t'ought dat you'd hug me up close.
   Go back, ol' buggah, you sha'n't have dis boy.
He ain't no tramp, ner no straggler, of co'se;
   He's pappy's pa'dner an' playmate an' joy.
Come to you' pallet now—go to yo' res';
   Wisht you could allus know ease an' cleah skies;
Wisht you could stay jes' a chile on my breas'—
   Little brown baby wif spa'klin' eyes!

Lover's Lane

   Summah night an' sighin' breeze
     'Long de lovah's lane;
   Frien'ly, shadder-mekin' trees,
     'Long de lovah's lane.

White folks' wo'k all done up gran'—
Me an' 'Mandy han'-in-han'
Struttin' lak we owned de lan',
    'Long de lovah's lane.

Owl a-settin' 'side de road,
    'Long de lovah's lane,
Lookin' at us lak he knowed
    Dis uz lovah's lane.
Go on, hoot yo' mou'nful tune,
You ain' nevah loved in June,
An' come hidin' f'om de moon
    Down in lovah's lane.

Bush it ben' an' nod an' sway,
    Down in lovah's lane,
Try'n' to hyeah me whut I say
    'Long de lovah's lane.
But I whispahs low lak dis,
An' my 'Mandy smile huh bliss—
Mistah Bush he shek his fis',
    Down in lovah's lane.

Whut I keer ef day is long,
    Down in lovah's lane.
I kin allus sing a song
    'Long de lovah's lane.
An' de wo'ds I hyeah an' say
Meks up fu' de weary day
W'en I's strollin' by de way,
    Down in lovah's lane.

An' dis t'ought will allus rise
    Down in lovah's lane;
Wondah whethah in de skies
    Dey's a lovah's lane.
Ef dey ain't, I tell you true,
'Ligion do look mighty blue,
'Cause I do' know whut I'd do
    'Dout a lovah's lane.

My Sort O' Man

I don't believe in 'ristercrats
  An' never did, you see;
The plain ol' homelike sorter folks
  Is good enough fur me.
O' course, I don't desire a man
  To be too tarnal rough,
But then, I think all folks should know
  When they air nice enough.

Now there is folks in this here world,
  From peasant up to king,
Who want to be so awful nice
  They overdo the thing.
That's jest the thing that makes me sick,
  An' quicker 'n a wink
I set it down that them same folks
  Ain't half so good 's you think.

I like to see a man dress nice,
  In clothes becomin' too;
I like to see a woman fix
  As women orter to do;
An' boys an' gals I like to see
  Look fresh an' young an' spry,—
We all must have our vanity
  An' pride before we die.

But I jedge no man by his clothes,—
  Nor gentleman nor tramp;
The man that wears the finest suit
  May be the biggest scamp,
An' he whose limbs air clad in rags
  That make a mournful sight,
In life's great battle may have proved
  A hero in the fight.

I don't believe in 'ristercrats;
  I like the honest tan

That lies upon the healthful cheek
   An' speaks the honest man;
I like to grasp the brawny hand
   That labor's lips have kissed,
For he who has not labored here
   Life's greatest pride has missed:

The pride to feel that yore own strength
   Has cleaved fur you the way
To heights to which you were not born,
   But struggled day by day.
What though the thousands sneer an' scoff,
   An' scorn yore humble birth?
Kings are but puppets; you are king
   By right o' royal worth.

The man who simply sits an' waits
   Fur good to come along,
Ain't worth the breath that one would take
   To tell him he is wrong.
Fur good ain't flowin' round this world
   Fur every fool to sup;
You've got to put yore see-ers on,
   An' go an' hunt it up.

Good goes with honesty, I say,
   To honour an' to bless;
To rich an' poor alike it brings
   A wealth o' happiness.
The 'ristercrats ain't got it all,
   Fur much to their su'prise,
That's one of earth's most blessed things
   They can't monopolize.

A Death Song

Lay me down beneaf de willers in de grass,
Whah de branch'll go a-singin' as it pass.
   An' w'en I's a-layin' low,

    I kin hyeah it as it go
Singin', "Sleep, my honey, tek yo' res' at las'."

Lay me nigh to whah hit meks a little pool,
An' de watah stan's so quiet lak an' cool,
    Whah de little birds in spring,
    Ust to come an' drink an' sing,
An' de chillen waded on dey way to school.

Let me settle w'en my shouldahs draps dey load
Nigh enough to hyeah de noises in de road;
    Fu' I t'ink de las' long res'
    Gwine to soothe my sperrit bes'
Ef I's layin' 'mong de t'ings I's allus knowed.

Dely

        Jes' lak toddy wahms you thoo'
            Sets yo' haid a reelin',
        Meks you ovah good and new,
            Dat's de way I's feelin'.
        Seems to me hit's summah time,
            Dough hit's wintah reely,
        I's a feelin' jes' dat prime—
            Ah' huh name is Dely.

        Dis hyeah love's a cu'rus thing,
            Changes 'roun' de season,
        Meks you sad or meks you sing,
            'Dout no urfly reason.
        Sometimes I go mopin' 'roun',
            Den agin I's leapin';
        Sperits allus up an' down
            Even when I's sleepin'.

        Fu' de dreams comes to me den,
            An' dey keeps me pitchin',
        Lak de apple dumplin's w'en
            Bilin' in de kitchen.

Some one sot to do me hahm,
    Tryin' to ovahcome me,
Ketchin' Dely by de ahm
    So's to tek huh f'om me.

Mon, you bettah b'lieve I fights
    (Dough hit's on'y seemin');
I's a hittin' fu' my rights
    Even w'en I's dreamin'.
But I'd let you have 'em all,
    Give 'em to you freely,
Good an' bad ones, great an' small,
    So's you leave me Dely.

Dely got dem meltin' eyes,
    Big an' black an' tendah.
Dely jes' a lady-size,
    Delikit an' slendah.
Dely brown ez brown kin be
    An' huh haih is curly;
Oh, she look so sweet to me, —
    Bless de precious girlie!

Dely brown ez brown kin be,
    She ain' no mullatter;
She pure cullud, — don' you see
    Dat's jes' whut's de mattah?
Dat's de why I love huh so,
    D' ain't no mix about huh,
Soon's you see huh face you know
    D' ain't no chanst to doubt huh.

Folks dey go to chu'ch an' pray
    So's to git a blessin'.
Oomph, dey bettah come my way,
    Dey could lu'n a lesson.
Sabbaf day I don' go fu',
    Jes' to see my pigeon;
I jes' sets an' looks at huh,
    Dat's enuff 'uligion.

A Letter

Dear Miss Lucy: I been t'inkin' dat I'd write you long fo' dis,
But dis writin' 's mighty tejous, an' you know jes' how it is.
But I's got a little lesure, so I teks my pen in han'
Fu' to let you know my feelin's since I retched dis furrin' lan'.
I's right well, I's glad to tell you (dough dis climate ain't to blame),
An' I hopes w'en dese lines reach you, dat dey'll fin' yo' se'f de same.
Cose I'se feelin' kin' o' homesick—dat's ez nachul ez kin be,
W'en a feller's mo'n th'ee thousand miles across dat awful sea.
(Don't you let nobidy fool you 'bout de ocean bein' gran';
If you want to see de billers, you jes' view dem f'om de lan'.)
'Bout de people? We been t'inkin' dat all white folks was alak;
But dese Englishmen is diffunt, an' dey's curus fu' a fac'.
Fust, dey's heavier an' redder in dey make-up an' dey looks,
An' dey don't put salt nor pepper in a blessed t'ing dey cooks!
W'en dey gin you good ol' tu'nips, ca'ots, pa'snips, beets, an' sich,
Ef dey ain't some one to tell you, you cain't 'stinguish which is which.
W'en I t'ought I's eatin' chicken—you may b'lieve dis hyeah's a lie—
But de waiter beat me down dat I was eatin' rabbit pie.
An' dey'd t'ink dat you was crazy—jes' a reg'lar ravin' loon,
Ef you'd speak erbout a 'possum or a piece o' good ol' coon.
O, hit's mighty nice, dis trav'lin', an' I's kin' o' glad I come.
But, I reckon, now I's willin' fu' to tek my way back home.
I done see de Crystal Palace, an' I's hyeahd dey string-band play,
But I hasn't seen no banjos layin' nowhahs 'roun' dis way.
Jes' gin ol' Jim Bowles a banjo, an' he'd not go very fu',
'Fo' he'd outplayed all dese fiddlers, wif dey flourish and dey stir.
Evahbiddy dat I's met wif has been monst'ous kin' an' good;
But I t'ink I'd lak it better to be down in Jones's wood,
Where we ust to have sich frolics, Lucy, you an' me an' Nelse,
Dough my appetite 'ud call me, ef dey wasn't nuffin else.
I'd jes' lak to have some sweet-pertaters roasted in de skin;
I's a-longin' fu' my chittlin's an' my mustard greens ergin;
I's a-wishin' fu' some buttermilk, an' co'n braid, good an' brown,
An' a drap o' good ol' bourbon fu' to wash my feelin's down!
An' I's comin' back to see you jes' as ehly as I kin,
So you better not go spa'kin' wif dat wuffless scoun'el Quin!
Well, I reckon, I mus' close now; write ez soon's dis reaches you;
Gi' my love to Sister Mandy an' to Uncle Isham, too.
Tell de folks I sen' 'em howdy; gin a kiss to pap an' mam;

Closin' I is, deah Miss Lucy,
   Still Yo' Own True-Lovin' SAM.
P.S. Ef you cain't mek out dis letter, lay it by erpon de she'f,
   An' when I git home, I'll read it, darlin', to you my own se'f.

A Cabin Tale

The Young Master Asks For a Story

Whut you say, dah? huh, uh! chile,
You's enough to dribe me wile.
Want a sto'y; jes' hyeah dat!
Whah' 'll I git a sto'y at?
Di'n' I tell you th'ee las' night?
Go 'way, honey, you ain't right.
I got somep'n' else to do,
'Cides jes' tellin' tales to you.
Tell you jes' one? Lem me see
Whut dat one's a-gwine to be.
When you's ole, yo membry fails;
Seems lak I do' know no tales.
Well, set down dah in dat cheer,
Keep still ef you wants to hyeah.
Tek dat chin up off yo' han's,
Set up nice now. Goodness lan's!
Hol' yo'se'f up lak yo' pa.
Bet nobidy evah saw
Him scrunched down lak you was den—
High-tone boys meks high-tone men.

   Once dey was a ole black bah,
Used to live 'roun' hyeah somewhah
In a cave. He was so big
He could ca'y off a pig
Lak you picks a chicken up,
Er yo' leetles' bit o' pup.
An' he had two gread big eyes,
Jes' erbout a saucer's size.
Why, dey looked lak balls o' fiah
Jumpin' 'roun' erpon a wiah
W'en dat bah was mad; an' laws!

But you ought to seen his paws!
Did I see 'em? How you 'spec
I's a-gwine to ricollec'
Dis hyeah ya'n I's try'n' to spin
Ef you keeps on puttin' in?
You keep still an' don't you cheep
Less I'll sen' you off to sleep.
Dis hyeah bah'd go trompin' 'roun'
Eatin' evahthing he foun';
No one couldn't have a fa'm
But dat bah 'u'd do 'em ha'm;
And dey couldn't ketch de scamp,
Anywhah he wan'ed to tramp.
Dah de scoun'el 'd mek his track,
Do his du't an' come on back.
He was sich a sly ole limb,
Traps was jes' lak fun to him.

   Now, down neah whah Mistah Bah
Lived, dey was a weasel dah;
But dey wasn't fren's a-tall
Case de weasel was so small.
An' de bah 'u'd, jes' fu' sass,
Tu'n his nose up w'en he'd pass.
Weasels's small o' cose, but my!
Dem air animiles is sly.
So dis hyeah one says, says he,
"I'll jes' fix dat bah, you see."
So he fixes up his plan
An' hunts up de fa'merman.
When de fa'mer see him come,
He 'mence lookin' mighty glum,
An' he ketches up a stick;
But de weasel speak up quick:
"Hol' on, Mistah Fa'mer man,
I wan' 'splain a little plan.
Ef you waits, I'll tell you whah
An' jes' how to ketch ol' Bah.
But I tell you now you mus'
Gin me one fat chicken fus'."
Den de man he scratch his haid,
Las' he say, "I'll mek de trade."

So de weasel et his hen,
Smacked his mouf and says, "Well, den,
Set yo' trap an' bait ternight,
An' I'll ketch de bah all right."
Den he ups an' goes to see
Mistah Bah, an' says, says he:
"Well, fren' Bah, we *ain't* been fren's,
But ternight ha'd feelin' en's.
Ef you ain't too proud to steal,
We kin git a splendid meal.
Cose I wouldn't come to you,
But it mus' be done by two;
Hit's a trap, but we kin beat
All dey tricks an' git de meat."
"Cose I's wif you," says de bah,
"Come on, weasel, show me whah."
Well, dey trots erlong ontwell
Dat air meat beginned to smell
In de trap. Den weasel say:
"Now you put yo' paw dis way
While I hol' de spring back so,
Den you grab de meat an' go."
Well, de bah he had to grin
Ez he put his big paw in,
Den he juked up, but—kerbing!
Weasel done let go de spring.
"Dah now," says de weasel, "dah,
I done cotched you, Mistah Bah!"
O, dat bah did sno't and spout,
Try'n' his bestes' to git out,
But de weasel say, "Goo'-bye!
Weasel small, but weasel sly."
Den he tu'ned his back an' run
Tol' de fa'mer whut he done.
So de fa'mer come down dah,
Wif a axe and killed de bah.

      Dah now, ain't dat sto'y fine?
Run erlong now, nevah min'.
Want some mo', you rascal, you?
No, suh! no, suh! dat'll do.

How Lucy Backslid

De times is mighty stirrin' 'mong de people up ouah way,
Dey 'sputin' an' dey argyin' an' fussin' night an' day;
An' all dis monst'ous trouble dat hit meks me tiahed to tell
Is 'bout dat Lucy Jackson dat was sich a mighty belle.

She was de preachah's favoured, an' he tol' de chu'ch one night
Dat she travelled thoo de cloud o' sin a-bearin' of a light;
But, now, I 'low he t'inkin' dat she mus' 'a' los' huh lamp,
Case Lucy done backslided an' dey trouble in de camp.

Huh daddy wants to beat huh, but huh mammy daihs him to,
Fu' she lookin' at de question f'om a ooman's pint o' view;
An' she say dat now she wouldn't have it diff'ent ef she could;
Dat huh darter only acted jes' lak any othah would.

Cose you know w'en women argy, dey is mighty easy led
By dey hea'ts an' don't go foolin' 'bout de reasons of de haid.
So huh mammy laid de law down (she ain' reckernizin' wrong),
But you got to mek erlowance fu' de cause dat go along.

Now de cause dat made Miss Lucy fu' to th'ow huh grace away
I's afeard won't baih no 'spection w'en hit come to jedgement day;
Do' de same t'ing been a-wo'kin' evah sence de worl' began,—
De ooman disobeyin' fu' to 'tice along a man.

Ef you 'tended de revivals which we held de wintah pas',
You kin rickolec' dat convuts was a—comin' thick an' fas';
But dey ain't no use in talkin', dey was all lef' in de lu'ch
W'en ol' Mis' Jackson's dartah foun' huh peace an' tuk de chu'ch.

W'y, she shouted ovah evah inch of Ebenezah's flo';
Up into de preachah's pulpit an' f'om dah down to de do';
Den she hugged an' squeezed huh mammy, an' she hugged an' kissed
    huh dad,
An' she struck out at huh sistah, people said, lak she was mad.

I has 'tended some revivals dat was lively in my day,
An' I's seed folks git 'uligion in mos' evah kin' o' way;
But I tell you, an' you b'lieve me dat I's speakin' true indeed,
Dat gal tuk huh 'ligion ha'dah dan de ha'dest yit I's seed.

Well, f'om dat, 't was "Sistah Jackson, won't you please do dis er dat?"
She mus' allus sta't de singin' w'en dey'd pass erroun' de hat,
An' hit seemed dey wasn't nuffin' in dat chu'ch dat could go by
'Dout sistah Lucy Jackson had a finger in de pie.

But de sayin' mighty trufeful dat hit easiah to sail
W'en de sea is ca'm an' gentle dan to weathah out a gale.
Dat's whut made dis ooman's trouble; ef de sto'm had kep' away,
She'd 'a' had enough 'uligion fu' to lasted out huh day.

Lucy went wid 'Lishy Davis, but w'en she jined chu'ch, you know
Dah was lots o' little places dat, of cose, she couldn't go;
An' she had to gin up dancin' an' huh singin' an' huh play. —
Now hit's nachul dat sich goin's-on 'u'd drive a man away.

So, w'en Lucy got so solemn, Ike he sta'ted fu' to go
Wid a gal who was a sinnah an' could mek a bettah show.
Lucy jes' went on to meetin' lak she didn't keer a rap,
But my 'sperunce kep' me t'inkin' dah was somep'n' gwine to drap.

Fu' a gal won't let 'uligion er no othah so't o' t'ing
Stop huh w'en she teks a notion dat she wants a weddin' ring.
You kin p'omise huh de blessin's of a happy aftah life
(An' hit's nice to be a angel), but she'd ravah be a wife.

So w'en Chrismus come an' mastah gin a frolic on de lawn,
Didn't 'sprise me not de littlest seein' Lucy lookin' on.
An' I seed a wa'nin' lightnin' go a-flashin' f'om huh eye
Jest ez 'Lishy an' his new gal went a-gallivantin' by.

An' dat Tildy, umph! she giggled, an' she gin huh dress a flirt
Lak de people she was passin' was ez common ez de dirt;
An' de minit she was dancin', w'y dat gal put on mo' aihs
Dan a cat a-tekin' kittens up a paih o' windin' staihs.

She could 'fo'd to show huh sma'tness, fu' she couldn't he'p but know
Dat wid jes' de present dancahs she was ownah of de flo';

But I t'ink she'd kin' o' cooled down ef she happened on de sly
Fu' to noticed dat 'ere lightnin' dat I seed in Lucy's eye.

An' she wouldn't been so 'stonished w'en de people gin a shout,
An' Lucy th'owed huh mantle back an' come a-glidin' out.
Some ahms was dah to tek huh an' she fluttahed down de flo'
Lak a feddah f'om a bedtick w'en de win' commence to blow.

Soon ez Tildy see de trouble, she jes' tu'n an' toss huh haid,
But seem lak she los' huh sperrit, all huh darin'ness was daid.
Didn't cut anothah capah nary time de blessid night;
But de othah one, hit looked lak couldn't git enough delight.

W'en you keeps a colt a-stan'nin' in de stable all along,
W'en he do git out hit's nachul he'll be pullin' mighty strong.
Ef you will tie up yo' feelin's, hyeah's de bes' advice to tek,
Look out fu' an awful loosin' w'en de string dat hol's 'em brek.

Lucy's mammy groaned to see huh, an' huh pappy sto'med an' to',
But she kep' right on a-hol'in' to de centah of de flo'.
So dey went an' ast de pastoh ef he couldn't mek huh quit,
But de tellin' of de sto'y th'owed de preachah in a fit.

Tildy Taylor chewed huh hank'cher twell she'd chewed it in a hole, —
All de sinnahs was rejoicin' 'cause a lamb had lef' de fol',
An' de las' I seed o' Lucy, she an' 'Lish was side an' side:
I don't blame de gal fu' dancin', an' I couldn't ef I tried.

Fu' de men dat wants to ma'y ain't a-growin' 'roun' on trees,
An' de gal dat wants to git one sholy has to try to please.
Hit's a ha'd t'ing fu' a ooman fu' to pray an' jes' set down,
An' to sacafice a husban' so's to try to gain a crown.

Now, I don' say she was justified in follerin' huh plan;
But aldough she los' huh 'ligion, yit she sholy got de man.
Latah on, w'en she is suttain dat de preachah's made 'em fas'
She kin jes' go back to chu'ch an' ax fu'giveness fu' de pas'!

Dinah Kneading Dough

I have seen full many a sight
Born of day or drawn by night:
Sunlight on a silver stream,
Golden lilies all a-dream,
Lofty mountains, bold and proud,
Veiled beneath the lacelike cloud;
But no lovely sight I know
Equals Dinah kneading dough.

Brown arms buried elbow-deep
Their domestic rhythm keep,
As with steady sweep they go
Through the gently yielding dough.
Maids may vaunt their finer charms—
Naught to me like Dinah's arms;
Girls may draw, or paint, or sew—
I love Dinah kneading dough.

Eyes of jet and teeth of pearl,
Hair, some say, too tight a-curl;
But the dainty maid I deem
Very near perfection's dream.
Swift she works, and only flings
Me a glance—the least of things.
And I wonder, does she know
That my heart is in the dough?

The Poet

He sang of life, serenely sweet,
    With, now and then, a deeper note.
    From some high peak, nigh yet remote,
He voiced the world's absorbing beat.

He sang of love when earth was young,
    And Love, itself, was in his lays.
    But ah, the world, it turned to praise
A jingle in a broken tongue.

Black Samson of Brandywine

"In the fight at Brandywine, Black Samson, a giant negro armed with a scythe, sweeps his way through the red ranks. . . ." C. M. Skinner's *"Myths and Legends of Our Own Land."*

Gray are the pages of record,
    Dim are the volumes of eld;
Else had old Delaware told us
    More that her history held.
Told us with pride in the story,
    Honest and noble and fine,
More of the tale of my hero,
    Black Samson of Brandywine.

Sing of your chiefs and your nobles,
    Saxon and Celt and Gaul,
Breath of mine ever shall join you,
    Highly I honor them all.
Give to them all of their glory,
    But for this noble of mine,
Lend him a tithe of your tribute,
    Black Samson of Brandywine.

There in the heat of the battle,
    There in the stir of the fight,
Loomed he, an ebony giant,
    Black as the pinions of night.
Swinging his scythe like a mower
    Over a field of grain,
Needless the care of the gleaners,
    Where he had passed amain.

Straight through the human harvest,
    Cutting a bloody swath,
Woe to you, soldier of Briton!
    Death is abroad in his path.
Flee from the scythe of the reaper,
    Flee while the moment is thine,
None may with safety withstand him,
    Black Samson of Brandywine.

Was he a freeman or bondman?
  Was he a man or a thing?
What does it matter? His brav'ry
  Renders him royal—a king.
If he was only a chattel,
  Honor the ransom may pay
Of the royal, the loyal black giant
  Who fought for his country that day.

Noble and bright is the story,
  Worthy the touch of the lyre,
Sculptor or poet should find it
  Full of the stuff to inspire.
Beat it in brass and in copper,
  Tell it in storied line,
So that the world may remember
  Black Samson of Brandywine.

Douglass

Ah, Douglass, we have fall'n on evil days,
  Such days as thou, not even thou didst know,
  When thee, the eyes of that harsh long ago
Saw, salient, at the cross of devious ways,
And all the country heard thee with amaze.
  Not ended then, the passionate ebb and flow,
  The awful tide that battled to and fro;
We ride amid a tempest of dispraise.

Now, when the waves of swift dissension swarm,
  And Honor, the strong pilot, lieth stark,
Oh, for thy voice high-sounding o'er the storm,
  For thy strong arm to guide the shivering bark,
The blast-defying power of thy form,
  To give us comfort through the lonely dark.

Slow Through the Dark

Slow moves the pageant of a climbing race;
   Their footsteps drag far, far below the height,
   And, unprevailing by their utmost might,
Seem faltering downward from each hard won place.
No strange, swift-sprung exception we; we trace
   A devious way thro' dim, uncertain light,—
   Our hope, through the long vistaed years, a sight
Of that our Captain's soul sees face to face.
   Who, faithless, faltering that the road is steep,
Now raiseth up his drear insistent cry?
   Who stoppeth here to spend a while in sleep
Or curseth that the storm obscures the sky?
   Heed not the darkness round you, dull and deep;
The clouds grow thickest when the summit's nigh.

Philosophy

I been t'inkin' 'bout de preachah; whut he said de othah night,
   'Bout hit bein' people's dooty, fu' to keep dey faces bright;
How one ought to live so pleasant dat ouah tempah never riles,
   Meetin' evahbody roun' us wid ouah very nicest smiles.

Dat's all right, I ain't a-sputin' not a t'ing dat soun's lak fac',
   But you don't ketch folks a-grinnin' wid a misery in de back;
An' you don't fin' dem a-smilin' w'en dey's hongry ez kin be,
   Leastways, dat's how human natur' allus seems to 'pear to me.

We is mos' all putty likely fu' to have our little cares,
   An' I think we's doin' fus' rate w'en we jes' go long and bears,
Widout breakin' up ouah faces in a sickly so't o' grin,
   W'en we knows dat in ouah innards we is p'intly mad ez sin.

Oh dey's times fu' bein' pleasant an' fu' goin' smilin' roun',
   'Cause I don't believe in people allus totin' roun' a frown,
But it's easy 'nough to titter w'en de stew is smokin' hot,
   But hit's mighty ha'd to giggle w'en dey's nuffin' in de pot.

On the Dedication of Dorothy Hall

Tuskegee, Ala., April 22, 1901.

Not to the midnight of the gloomy past,
    Do we revert to-day; we look upon
The golden present and the future vast
    Whose vistas show us visions of the dawn.

Nor shall the sorrows of departed years
    The sweetness of our tranquil souls annoy,
The sunshine of our hopes dispels the tears,
    And clears our eyes to see this later joy.

Not ever in the years that God hath given
    Have we gone friendless down the thorny way,
Always the clouds of pregnant black were riven
    By flashes from His own eternal day.

The women of a race should be its pride;
    We glory in the strength our mothers had,
We glory that this strength was not denied
    To labor bravely, nobly, and be glad.

God give to these within this temple here,
    Clear vision of the dignity of toil,
That virtue in them may its blossoms rear
    Unspotted, fragrant, from the lowly soil.

God bless the givers for their noble deed,
    Shine on them with the mercy of Thy face,
Who come with open hearts to help and speed
    The striving women of a struggling race.

To the South

On Its New Slavery

Heart of the Southland, heed me pleading now,
Who bearest, unashamed, upon my brow
The long kiss of the loving tropic sun,
And yet, whose veins with thy red current run.

Borne on the bitter winds from every hand,
Strange tales are flying over all the land,
And Condemnation, with his pinions foul,
Glooms in the place where broods the midnight owl.

What art thou, that the world should point at thee,
And vaunt and chide the weakness that they see?
There was a time they were not wont to chide;
Where is thy old, uncompromising pride?

Blood-washed, thou shouldst lift up thine honored head,
White with the sorrow for thy loyal dead
Who lie on every plain, on every hill,
And whose high spirit walks the Southland still:

Whose infancy our mother's hands have nursed.
Thy manhood, gone to battle unaccursed,
Our fathers left to till th' reluctant field,
To rape the soil for what she would not yield;

Wooing for aye, the cold unam'rous sod,
Whose growth for them still meant a master's rod;
Tearing her bosom for the wealth that gave
The strength that made the toiler still a slave.

Too long we hear the deep impassioned cry
That echoes vainly to the heedless sky;
Too long, too long, the Macedonian call
Falls fainting far beyond the outward wall,

Within whose sweep, beneath the shadowing trees,
A slumbering nation takes its dangerous ease;
Too long the rumors of thy hatred go
For those who loved thee and thy children so.

Thou must arise forthwith, and strong, thou must
Throw off the smirching of this baser dust,
Lay by the practice of this later creed,
And be thine honest self again indeed.

There was a time when even slavery's chain
Held in some joys to alternate with pain,
Some little light to give the night relief,
Some little smiles to take the place of grief.

There was a time when, jocund as the day,
The toiler hoed his row and sung his lay,
Found something gleeful in the very air,
And solace for his toiling everywhere.

Now all is changed, within the rude stockade,
A bondsman whom the greed of men has made
Almost too brutish to deplore his plight,
Toils hopeless on from joyless morn till night.

For him no more the cabin's quiet rest,
The homely joys that gave to labor zest;
No more for him the merry banjo's sound,
Nor trip of lightsome dances footing round.

For him no more the lamp shall glow at eve,
Nor chubby children pluck him by the sleeve;
No more for him the master's eyes be bright,—
He has nor freedom's nor a slave's delight.

What, was it all for naught, those awful years
That drenched a groaning land with blood and tears?
Was it to leave this sly convenient hell,
That brother fighting his own brother fell?

When that great struggle held the world in awe,
And all the nations blanched at what they saw,
Did Sanctioned Slavery bow its conquered head
That this unsanctioned crime might rise instead?

Is it for this we all have felt the flame,—
This newer bondage and this deeper shame?
Nay, not for this, a nation's heroes bled,
And North and South with tears beheld their dead.

Oh, Mother South, hast thou forgot thy ways,
Forgot the glory of thine ancient days,
Forgot the honor that once made thee great,
And stooped to this unhallowed estate?

It cannot last, thou wilt come forth in might,
A warrior queen full armored for the fight;
And thou wilt take, e'en with thy spear in rest,
Thy dusky children to thy saving breast.

Till then, no more, no more the gladsome song,
Strike only deeper chords, the notes of wrong;
Till then, the sigh, the tear, the oath, the moan,
Till thou, oh, South, and thine, come to thine own.

The Haunted Oak

Pray why are you so bare, so bare,
    Oh, bough of the old oak-tree;
And why, when I go through the shade you throw,
    Runs a shudder over me?

My leaves were green as the best, I trow,
    And sap ran free in my veins,
But I saw in the moonlight dim and weird
    A guiltless victim's pains.

I bent me down to hear his sigh;
    I shook with his gurgling moan,
And I trembled sore when they rode away,
    And left him here alone.

They'd charged him with the old, old crime,
    And set him fast in jail:
Oh, why does the dog howl all night long,
    And why does the night wind wail?

He prayed his prayer and he swore his oath,
    And he raised his hand to the sky;

But the beat of hoofs smote on his ear,
   And the steady tread drew nigh.

Who is it rides by night, by night,
   Over the moonlit road?
And what is the spur that keeps the pace,
   What is the galling goad?

And now they beat at the prison door,
   "Ho, keeper, do not stay!
We are friends of him whom you hold within,
   And we fain would take him away

"From those who ride fast on our heels
   With mind to do him wrong;
They have no care for his innocence,
   And the rope they bear is long."

They have fooled the jailer with lying words,
   They have fooled the man with lies;
The bolts unbar, the locks are drawn,
   And the great door open flies.

Now they have taken him from the jail,
   And hard and fast they ride,
And the leader laughs low down in his throat,
   As they halt my trunk beside.

Oh, the judge, he wore a mask of black,
   And the doctor one of white,
And the minister, with his oldest son,
   Was curiously bedight.

Oh, foolish man, why weep you now?
   'T is but a little space,
And the time will come when these shall dread
   The mem'ry of your face.

I feel the rope against my bark,
   And the weight of him in my grain,

I feel in the throe of his final woe
  The touch of my own last pain.

And never more shall leaves come forth
  On a bough that bears the ban;
I am burned with dread, I am dried and dead,
  From the curse of a guiltless man.

And ever the judge rides by, rides by,
  And goes to hunt the deer,
And ever another rides his soul
  In the guise of a mortal fear.

And ever the man he rides me hard,
  And never a night stays he;
For I feel his curse as a haunted bough,
  On the trunk of a haunted tree.

The Unsung Heroes

A song for the unsung heroes who rose in the country's need,
When the life of the land was threatened by the slaver's cruel greed,
For the men who came from the cornfield, who came from the plough
    and the flail,
Who rallied round when they heard the sound of the mighty man of
    the rail.

They laid them down in the valleys, they laid them down in the wood,
And the world looked on at the work they did, and whispered, "It is
    good."
They fought their way on the hillside, they fought their way in the glen,
And God looked down on their sinews brown, and said, "I have made
    them men."

They went to the blue lines gladly, and the blue lines took them in,
And the men who saw their muskets' fire thought not of their dusky
    skin.

The gray lines rose and melted beneath their scathing showers,
And they said, "'T is true, they have force to do, these old slave boys of
    ours."

Ah, Wagner saw their glory, and Pillow knew their blood,
That poured on a nation's altar, a sacrificial flood.
Port Hudson heard their war-cry that smote its smoke-filled air,
And the old free fires of their savage sires again were kindled there.

They laid them down where the rivers the greening valleys gem.
And the song of the thund'rous cannon was their sole requiem,
And the great smoke wreath that mingled its hue with the dusky cloud,
Was the flag that furled o'er a saddened world, and the sheet that made
    their shroud.

Oh, Mighty God of the Battles Who held them in Thy hand,
Who gave them strength through the whole day's length, to fight for
    their native land,
They are lying dead on the hillsides, they are lying dead on the plain,
And we have not fire to smite the lyre and sing them one brief strain.

Give, Thou, some seer the power to sing them in their might,
The men who feared the master's whip, but did not fear the fight;
That he may tell of their virtues as minstrels did of old,
Till the pride of face and the hate of race grow obsolete and cold.

A song for the unsung heroes who stood the awful test,
When the humblest host that the land could boast went forth to meet
    the best;
A song for the unsung heroes who fell on the bloody sod,
Who fought their way from night to day and struggled up to God.

Resignation

Long had I grieved at what I deemed abuse;
    But now I am as grain within the mill.
If so be thou must crush me for thy use,
    Grind on, O potent God, and do thy will!

Robert Gould Shaw

Why was it that the thunder voice of Fate
    Should call thee, studious, from the classic groves,
    Where calm-eyed Pallas with still footstep roves,
And charge thee seek the turmoil of the state?
What bade thee hear the voice and rise elate,
    Leave home and kindred and thy spicy loaves,
    To lead th' unlettered and despised droves
To manhood's home and thunder at the gate?

Far better the slow blaze of Learning's light,
    The cool and quiet of her dearer fane,
Than this hot terror of a hopeless fight,
    This cold endurance of the final pain,—
Since thou and those who with thee died for right
    Have died, the Present teaches, but in vain!

Life's Tragedy

It may be misery not to sing at all
    And to go silent through the brimming day.
It may be sorrow never to be loved,
    But deeper griefs than these beset the way.

To have come near to sing the perfect song
    And only by a half-tone lost the key,
There is the potent sorrow, there the grief,
    The pale, sad staring of life's tragedy.

To have just missed the perfect love,
    Not the hot passion of untempered youth,
But that which lays aside its vanity
    And gives thee, for thy trusting worship, truth—

This, this it is to be accursed indeed;
    For if we mortals love, or if we sing,
We count our joys not by the things we have,
    But by what kept us from the perfect thing.

Compensation

Because I had loved so deeply,
    Because I had loved so long,
God in His great compassion
    Gave me the gift of song.

Because I have loved so vainly,
    And sung with such faltering breath,
The Master in infinite mercy
    Offers the boon of Death.

When Dey 'Listed Colored Soldiers

Dey was talkin' in de cabin, dey was talkin' in de hall;
But I listened kin' o' keerless, not a-t'inkin' 'bout it all;
An' on Sunday, too, I noticed, dey was whisp'rin' mighty much,
Stan'in' all erroun' de roadside w'en dey let us out o' chu'ch.
But I didn't t'ink erbout it 'twell de middle of de week,
An' my 'Lias come to see me, an' somehow he couldn't speak.
Den I seed all in a minute whut he'd come to see me for;—
Dey had 'listed colo'ed sojers an' my 'Lias gwine to wah.

Oh, I hugged him, an' I kissed him, an' I baiged him not to go;
But he tol' me dat his conscience, hit was callin' to him so,
An' he couldn't baih to lingah w'en he had a chanst to fight
For de freedom dey had gin him an' de glory of de right.
So he kissed me, an' he lef' me, w'en I'd p'omised to be true;
An' dey put a knapsack on him, an' a coat all colo'ed blue.
So I gin him pap's ol' Bible f'om de bottom of de draw',—
W'en dey 'listed colo'ed sojers an' my 'Lias went to wah.

But I t'ought of all de weary miles dat he would have to tramp,
An' I couldn't be contented w'en dey tuk him to de camp.
W'y my hea't nigh broke wid grievin' 'twell I seed him on de street;
Den I felt lak I could go an' th'ow my body at his feet.
For his buttons was a-shinin', an' his face was shinin', too,
An' he looked so strong an' mighty in his coat o' sojer blue,
Dat I hollahed, "Step up, manny," dough my th'oat was so' an' raw,—
W'en dey 'listed colo'ed sojers an' my 'Lias went to wah.

Ol' Mis' cried w'en mastah lef' huh, young Miss mou'ned huh brothah
    Ned,
An' I didn't know dey feelin's is de ve'y wo'ds dey said
W'en I tol' 'em I was so'y. Dey had done gin up dey all;
But dey only seemed mo' proudah dat dey men had hyeahed de call.
Bofe my mastahs went in gray suits, an' I loved de Yankee blue,
But I t'ought dat I could sorrer for de losin' of 'em too;
But I couldn't, for I didn't know de ha'f o' whut I saw,
'Twell dey 'listed colo'ed sojers an' my 'Lias went to wah.

Mastah Jack come home all sickly; he was broke for life, dey said;
An' dey lef' my po' young mastah some'r's on de roadside,—dead.
W'en de women cried an' mou'ned 'em, I could feel it thoo an' thoo,
For I had a loved un fightin' in de way o' dangah, too.
Den dey tol' me dey had laid him some'r's way down souf to res',
Wid de flag dat he had fit for shinin' daih acrost his breas'.
Well, I cried, but den I reckon dat's whut Gawd had called him for,
W'en dey 'listed colo'ed sojers an' my 'Lias went to wah.

De Way T'ings Come

De way t'ings come, hit seems to me,
Is des' one monst'ous mystery;
De way hit seem to strike a man,
De ain't no sense, dey ain't no plan;
Ef trouble sta'ts a pilin' down,
It ain't no use to rage er frown,
It ain't no use to strive er pray,
Hit's mortal boun' to come dat way.

Now, ef you's hongry, an' yo' plate
Des' keep on sayin' to you, "Wait,"
Don't mek no diffunce how you feel,
'T won't do no good to hunt a meal,
Fu' dat ah meal des' boun' to hide
Ontwell de devil's satisfied,
An' 'twell dey's somep'n by to cyave
You's got to ease yo'se'f an' sta've.

But ef dey's co'n meal on de she'f
You needn't bothah 'roun' yo'se'f,
Somebody's boun' to amble in
An' 'vite you to dey co'n meal bin;
An' ef you's stuffed up to de froat
Wid co'n er middlin', fowl er shoat,
Des' look out an' you'll see fu' sho'
A 'possum faint befo' yo' do'.

De way t'ings happen, huhuh, chile,
Dis worl' 's done puzzled me one w'ile;
I's mighty skeered I'll fall in doubt,
I des' won't try to reason out
De reason why folks strive an' plan
A dinnah fu' a full-fed man,
An' shet de do' an' cross de street
F''om one dat raaly needs to eat.

Temptation

I done got 'uligion, honey, an' I's happy ez a king;
Evahthing I see erbout me's jes' lak sunshine in de spring;
An' it seems lak I do' want to do anothah blessid thing
But jes' run an' tell de neighbours, an' to shout an' pray an' sing.

I done shuk my fis' at Satan, an' I's gin de worl' my back;
I do' want no hendrin' causes now a-both'rin' in my track;
Fu' I's on my way to glory, an' I feels too sho' to miss.
W'y, dey ain't no use in sinnin' when 'uligion's sweet ez dis.

Talk erbout a man backslidin' w'en he's on de gospel way;
No, suh, I done beat de debbil, an' Temptation's los' de day.
Gwine to keep my eyes right straight up, gwine to shet my eahs, an' see
Whut ole projick Mistah Satan's gwine to try to wuk on me.

Listen, whut dat soun' I hyeah dah? 'tain't no one commence to sing;
It's a fiddle; git erway dah! don' you hyeah dat blessid thing?
W'y, dat's sweet ez drippin' honey, 'cause, you knows, I draws de bow,
An' when music's sho' 'nough music, I's de one dat's sho' to know.

W'y, I's done de double shuffle, twell a body couldn't res',
Jes' a-hyeahin' Sam de fiddlah play dat chune his level bes';
I could cut a mighty caper, I could gin a mighty fling
Jes' right now, I's mo' dan suttain I could cut de pigeon wing.

Look hyeah, whut's dis I's been sayin'? whut on urf's tuk holt o' me?
Dat ole music come nigh runnin' my 'uligion up a tree!
Cleah out wif dat dah ole fiddle, don' you try dat trick agin;
Didn't think I could be tempted, but you lak to made me sin!

A Plea

Treat me nice, Miss Mandy Jane,
   Treat me nice.
Dough my love has tu'ned my brain,
   Treat me nice.
I ain't done a t'ing to shame,
Lovahs all ac's jes' de same:
Don't you know we ain't to blame?
   Treat me nice!

Cose I know I's talkin' wild;
   Treat me nice;
I cain't talk no bettah, child,
   Treat me nice;
Whut a pusson gwine to do,
W'en he come a-cou'tin' you
All a-trimblin' thoo and thoo?
   Please be nice.

Reckon I mus' go de paf
   Othahs do:
Lovahs lingah, ladies laff;
   Mebbe you
Do' mean all the things you say,
An' pu'haps some latah day
W'en I baig you ha'd, you may
   Treat me nice!

Chrismus on the Plantation

It was Chrismus Eve, I mind hit fu' a mighty gloomy day—
Bofe de weathah an' de people—not a one of us was gay;
Cose you'll t'ink dat's mighty funny 'twell I try to mek hit cleah,
Fu' a da'ky's allus happy when de holidays is neah.

But we wasn't, fu' dat mo'nin' Mastah'd tol' us we mus' go,
He'd been payin' us sence freedom, but he couldn't pay no mo';
He wa'n't nevah used to plannin' 'fo' he got so po' an' ol',
So he gwine to give up tryin', an' de homestead mus' be sol'.

I kin see him stan'in' now erpon de step ez cleah ez day,
Wid de win' a-kind o' fondlin' thoo his haih all thin an' gray;
An' I 'membah how he trimbled when he said, "It's ha'd fu' me,
Not to mek yo' Chrismus brightah, but I 'low it wa'n't to be."

All de women was a-cryin', an' de men, too, on de sly,
An' I noticed somep'n shinin' even in ol' Mastah's eye.
But we all stood still to listen ez ol' Ben come f'om de crowd
An' spoke up, a-try'n' to steady down his voice and mek it loud:—

"Look hyeah, Mastah, I's been servin' yo' fu' lo! dese many yeahs,
An' now, sence we's got freedom an' you's kind o' po', hit 'pears
Dat you want us all to leave you 'cause you don't t'ink you can pay.
Ef my membry hasn't fooled me, seem dat whut I hyead you say.

"Er in othah wo'ds, you wants us to fu'git dat you's been kin',
An' ez soon ez you is he'pless, we's to leave you hyeah behin'.
Well, ef dat's de way dis freedom ac's on people, white er black,
You kin jes' tell Mistah Lincum fu' to tek his freedom back.

"We gwine wo'k dis ol' plantation fu' whatevah we kin git,
Fu' I know hit did suppo't us, an' de place kin do it yit.
Now de land is yo's, de hands is ouahs, an' I reckon we'll be brave,
An' we'll bah ez much ez you do w'en we has to scrape an' save."

Ol' Mastah stood dah trimblin', but a-smilin' thoo his teahs,
An' den hit seemed jes' nachul-like, de place fah rung wid cheahs,
An' soon ez dey was quiet, some one sta'ted sof' an' low:
"Praise God," an' den we all jined in, "from whom all blessin's flow!"

Well, dey wasn't no use tryin', ouah min's was sot to stay,
An' po' ol' Mastah couldn't plead ner baig, ner drive us 'way,
An' all at once, hit seemed to us, de day was bright agin,
So evahone was gay dat night, an' watched de Chrismus in.

Theology

There is a heaven, for ever, day by day,
The upward longing of my soul doth tell me so.
There is a hell, I'm quite as sure; for pray,
If there were not, where would my neighbours go?

Li'l' Gal

Oh, de weathah it is balmy an' de breeze is sighin' low.
        Li'l' gal,
An' de mockin' bird is singin' in de locus' by de do',
        Li'l' gal;
Dere's a hummin' an' a bummin' in de lan' f'om eas' to wes',
I's a-sighin' fu' you, honey, an' I nevah know no res'.
Fu' dey's lots o' trouble brewin' an' a-stewin' in my breas',
        Li'l' gal.

Whut's de mattah wid de weathah, whut's de mattah wid de breeze,
        Li'l' gal?
Whut's de mattah wid de locus' dat's a-singin' in de trees,
        Li'l' gal?
W'y dey knows dey ladies love 'em, an' dey knows dey love 'em true,
An' dey love 'em back, I reckon, des' lak I's a-lovin' you;
Dat's de reason dey's a-weavin' an' a-sighin', thoo an' thoo,
        Li'l' gal.

Don't you let no da'ky fool you 'cause de clo'es he waihs is fine,
        Li'l' gal.
Dey's a hones' hea't a-beatin' unnerneaf dese rags o' mine,
        Li'l' gal.
Co'se dey ain' no use in mockin' whut de birds an' weathah do.
But I's so'y I cain't 'spress it w'en I knows I loves you true,
Dat's de reason I's a-sighin' an' a-singin' now fu' you,
        Li'l' gal.

The Old Cabin

In de dead of night I sometimes
   Git to t'inkin' of de pas'
An' de days w'en slavery helt me
   In my mis'ry—ha'd an' fas'.
Dough de time was mighty tryin',
   In dese houahs somehow hit seem
Dat a brightah light come slippin'
   Thoo de kivahs of my dream.

An' my min' fu'gits de whuppins,
   Draps de feah o' block an' lash
An' flies straight to somep'n' joyful
   In a secon's lightnin' flash.
Den hit seems I see a vision
   Of a dearah long ago
Of de childern tumblin' roun' me
   By my rough ol' cabin do'.

Talk about yo' go'geous mansions
   An' yo' big house great an' gran',
Des bring up de fines' palace
   Dat you know in all de lan'.
But dey's somep'n' dearah to me,
   Somep'n' faihah to my eyes
In dat cabin, less you bring me
   To yo' mansion in de skies.

I kin see de light a-shinin'
   Thoo de chinks atween de logs,
I kin hyeah de way-off bayin'
   Of my mastah's huntin' dogs,
An' de neighin' of de hosses
   Stampin' on de ol' bahn flo',
But above dese soun's de laughin'
   At my deah ol' cabin do'.

We would gethah daih at evenin',
   All my frien's 'ud come erroun'
An' hit wan't no time, twell, bless you,

You could hyeah de banjo's soun'.
You could see de dahkies dancin'
     Pigeon wing an' heel an' toe—
Joyous times I tell you people
     Roun' dat same ol' cabin do'.

But at times my t'oughts git saddah,
     Ez I riccolec' de folks,
An' dey frolickin' an' talkin'
     Wid dey laughin' an dey jokes.
An' hit hu'ts me w'en I membahs
     Dat I'll nevah see no mo'
Dem ah faces gethered smilin'
     Roun' dat po' ol' cabin do'.

Angelina

When de fiddle gits to singin' out a ol' Vahginny reel,
An' you 'mence to feel a ticklin' in yo' toe an' in yo' heel;
Ef you t'ink you got 'uligion an' you wants to keep it, too,
You jes' bettah tek a hint an' git yo'self clean out o' view.
Case de time is mighty temptin' when de chune is in de swing,
Fu' a darky, saint or sinner man, to cut de pigeon-wing.
An' you couldn't he'p f'om dancin' ef yo' feet was boun' wif twine,
When Angelina Johnson comes a-swingin' down de line.

Don't you know Miss Angelina? She's de da'lin' of de place.
W'y, dey ain't no high-toned lady wif sich mannahs an' sich grace.
She kin move across de cabin, wif its planks all rough an' wo';
Jes' de same's ef she was dancin' on ol' mistus' ball-room flo'.
Fact is, you do' see no cabin—evaht'ing you see look grand,
An' dat one ol' squeaky fiddle soun' to you jes' lak a ban';
Cotton britches look lak broadclof an' a linsey dress look fine,
When Angelina Johnson comes a-swingin' down de line.

Some folks say dat dancin's sinful, an' de blessed Lawd, dey say,
Gwine to punish us fu' steppin' w'en we hyeah de music play.
But I tell you I don' b'lieve it, fu' de Lawd is wise and good,
An' he made de banjo's metal an' he made de fiddle's wood,
An' he made de music in dem, so I don' quite t'ink he'll keer

Ef our feet keeps time a little to de melodies we hyeah.
W'y, dey's somep'n' downright holy in de way our faces shine,
When Angelina Johnson comes a-swingin' down de line.

Angelina steps so gentle, Angelina bows so low,
An' she lif' huh sku't so dainty dat huh shoetop skacely show:
An' dem teef o' huh'n a-shinin', ez she tek you by de han'—
Go 'way, people, d' ain't anothah sich a lady in de lan'!
When she's movin' thoo de figgers er a-dancin' by huhse'f,
Folks jes' stan' stock-still a-sta'in', an' dey mos' nigh hol's dey bref;
An' de young mens, dey's a-sayin', "I's gwine mek dat damsel mine,"
When Angelina Johnson comes a-swingin' down de line.

Weltschmerz

You ask why I am sad to-day,
I have no cares, no griefs, you say?
Ah, yes, 't is true, I have no grief—
But—is there not the falling leaf?

The bare tree there is mourning left
With all of autumn's gray bereft;
It is not what has happened me,
Think of the bare, dismantled tree.

The birds go South along the sky,
I hear their lingering, long good-bye.
Who goes reluctant from my breast?
And yet—the lone and windswept nest.

The mourning, pale-flowered hearse goes by,
Why does a tear come to my eye?
Is it the March rain blowing wild?
I have no dead, I know no child.

I am no widow by the bier
Of him I held supremely dear.
I have not seen the choicest one
Sink down as sinks the westering sun.

Faith unto faith have I beheld,
For me, few solemn notes have swelled;
Love beckoned me out to the dawn,
And happily I followed on.

And yet my heart goes out to them
Whose sorrow is their diadem;
The falling leaf, the crying bird,
The voice to be, all lost, unheard—

Not mine, not mine, and yet too much
The thrilling power of human touch,
While all the world looks on and scorns
I wear another's crown of thorns.

Count me a priest who understands
The glorious pain of nail-pierced hands;
Count me a comrade of the thief
Hot driven into late belief.

Oh, mother's tear, oh, father's sigh,
Oh, mourning sweetheart's last good-bye,
I yet have known no mourning save
Beside some brother's brother's grave.

Misapprehension

Out of my heart, one day, I wrote a song,
    With my heart's blood imbued,
Instinct with passion, tremulously strong,
    With grief subdued;
    Breathing a fortitude
        Pain-bought.
And one who claimed much love for what I wrought,
    Read and considered it,
        And spoke:
"Ay, brother,—'tis well writ,
    But where's the joke?"

A Plantation Melody

De trees is bendin' in de sto'm,
De rain done hid de mountain's fo'm,
   I's 'lone an' in distress.
But listen, dah's a voice I hyeah,
A-sayin' to me, loud an' cleah,
   "Lay low in de wildaness."

De lightnin' flash, de bough sway low,
My po' sick hea't is trimblin' so,
   It hu'ts my very breas'.
But him dat give de lightnin' powah
Jes' bids me in de tryin' howah
   "Lay low in de wildaness."

O brothah, w'en de tempes' beat,
An' w'en yo' weary head an' feet
   Can't fin' no place to res',
Jes' 'membah dat de Mastah's nigh,
An' putty soon you'll hyeah de cry,
   "Lay low in de wildaness."

O sistah, w'en de rain come down,
An' all yo' hopes is 'bout to drown,
   Don't trus' de Mastah less.
He smilin' w'en you t'ink he frown,
He ain' gwine let yo' soul sink down—
   Lay low in de wildaness.

Possum

Ef dey's anyt'ing dat riles me
   An' jes' gits me out o' hitch,
Twell I want to tek my coat off,
   So's to r'ar an' t'ar an' pitch,
Hit's to see some ign'ant white man
   'Mittin' dat owdacious sin—
W'en he want to cook a possum
   Tekin' off de possum's skin.

W'y dey ain't no use in talkin',
    Hit jes' hu'ts me to de hea't
Fu' to see dem foolish people
    Th'owin' 'way de fines' pa't.
W'y, dat skin is jes' ez tendah
    An' ez juicy ez kin be;
I knows all erbout de critter—
    Hide an' haih—don't talk to me!

Possum skin is jes' lak shoat skin;
    Jes' you swinge an' scrope it down,
Tek a good sha'p knife an' sco' it,
    Den you bake it good an' brown.
Huh-uh! honey, you's so happy
    Dat yo' thoughts is 'mos' a sin
When you's settin' dah a-chawin'
    On dat possum's cracklin' skin.

White folks t'ink dey know 'bout eatin',
    An' I reckon dat dey do
Sometimes git a little idee
    Of a middlin' dish er two;
But dey ain't a t'ing dey knows of
    Dat I reckon cain't be beat
W'en we set down at de table
    To a unskun possum's meat!

Parted

She wrapped her soul in a lace of lies,
    With a prime deceit to pin it;
And I thought I was gaining a fearsome prize,
    So I staked my soul to win it.

We wed and parted on her complaint,
    And both were a bit of barter,
Tho' I'll confess that I'm no saint,
    I'll swear that she's no martyr.

Right's Security

What if the wind do howl without,
And turn the creaking weathervane;
What if the arrows of the rain
Do beat against the window-pane?
Art thou not armored strong and fast
Against the sallies of the blast?
Art thou not sheltered safe and well
Against the flood's insistent swell?

What boots it, that thou stand'st alone,
And laughest in the battle's face
When all the weak have fled the place
And let their feet and fears keep pace?
Thou wavest still thine ensign, high,
And shoutest thy loud battle-cry;
Higher than e'er the tempest roared,
It cleaves the silence like a sword.

Right arms and armors, too, that man
Who will not compromise with wrong;
Though single, he must front the throng,
And wage the battle hard and long.
Minorities, since time began,
Have shown the better side of man;
And often in the lists of Time
One man has made a cause sublime!

Worn Out

You bid me hold my peace
　　And dry my fruitless tears,
Forgetting that I bear
　　A pain beyond my years.

You say that I should smile
　　And drive the gloom away;
I would, but sun and smiles
　　Have left my life's dark day.

All time seems cold and void,
    And naught but tears remain;
Life's music beats for me
    A melancholy strain.

I used at first to hope,
    But hope is past and gone;
And now without a ray
    My cheerless life drags on.

Like to an ash-stained hearth
    When all its fires are spent;
Like to an autumn wood
    By storm winds rudely shent,—

So sadly goes my heart,
    Unclothed of hope and peace;
It asks not joy again,
    But only seeks release.

Silence

'T is better to sit here beside the sea,
    Here on the spray-kissed beach,
In silence, that between such friends as we
    Is full of deepest speech.

A Song

Thou art the soul of a summer's day,
Thou art the breath of the rose.
    But the summer is fled
    And the rose is dead;
Where are they gone, who knows, who knows?

Thou art the blood of my heart o' hearts,
Thou art my soul's repose,
    But my heart grows numb

    And my soul is dumb;
Where art thou, love, who knows, who knows?

Thou art the hope of my after years—
Sun for my winter snows;
    But the years go by
    'Neath a clouded sky.
Where shall we meet, who knows, who knows?

Index of Titles and First Lines